1 ABOUT THE AUTHOR

Publishers like to print information about the author of a book inside the book's cover. Write a brief biography of yourself to be included inside each book you write.

You may wish to include a self-portrait.

5 FAMILY FUN

Name ....

Bertie Blob is an orphan who wants his own family. Make up a family for him and describe them.

BERTIE'S MUM
BERTIE'S DAD
BERTIE BLOB
Bertie Blob is a real slob he only eats green jelly and he lives in a garbage bin. He likes to chase cats and

6 SCHOOL RULES

Name . . . .

You have been appointed to write a set of rules for your school. Write down the rules which you think are the most important and explain why you think they are important.

Discuss your rules with your friends. Decide which rules your school should adopt.

7 EASTER SYMBOLS

Name . . . .

Research to find out all you can about one of the symbols of Easter. Write a report explaining what your symbol represents and why it is significant.

8 BE THE BUNNY

Name. . . . .

You have a part-time job as the Easter Bunny in your local shopping centre. Imagine spending a day in that heavy, hot suit being followed around by all those little children. Write about your worst or funniest day.

9 PERSONAL LETTER

Name ....

Use this piece of writing paper to write to a friend. You must use the format on the sheet.

....

....

....

....

....

....

....

....

....

....

....

....

....

....

....

....

....

....

....

....

....

....

10 ADDRESSING

Name . . . .

Make up this envelope and use it to send a letter or an invitation.

Directions

1. Cut out the envelope.
2. Fold dotted lines marked A in.
3. Fold dotted line marked B.
4. Glue the B flap to the tabs at the side of the envelope.
5. Fold the flap over along the dotted line marked C.
6. Use the model to address your envelope correctly.

Don't forget the postcode.

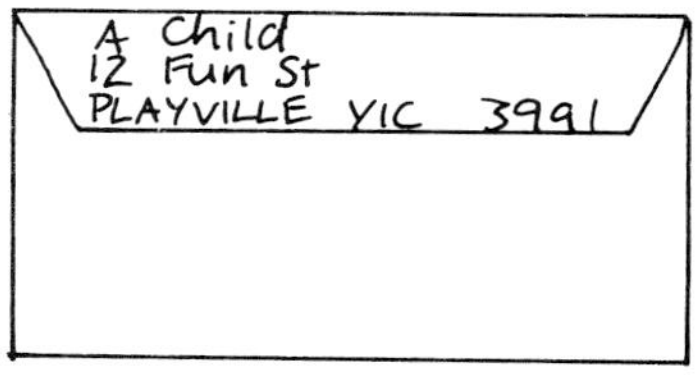

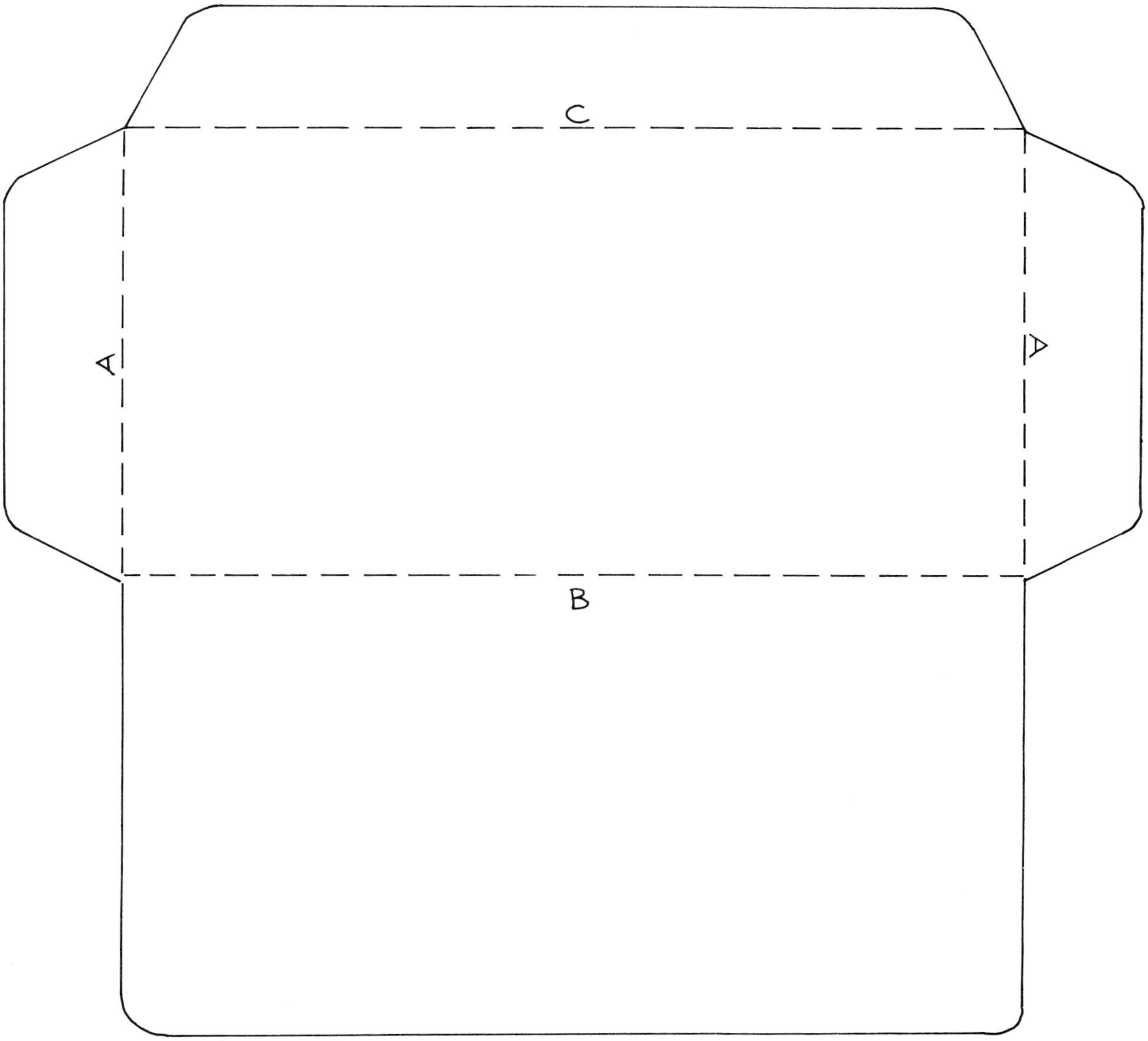

11 VIBRANT VITAMINS

Name ....

You have invented a new vitamin pill. Its uses are unlimited. Design a label for the jar which will tell people what these vitamins will do for them.

12 MOTHER'S AWARD

Name . . . .

Design an award to be presented on Mother's Day.

You will need to explain who the award is being given to and why.

13 IMAGES OF AUTUMN

Name ....

Fill this leaf with as many Autumn words as you can think of.

Choose 14 of the words to make into a poem.

Arrange the words to make a pattern with four lines:

the first line has 3 words;

the second line has 4 words;

the third line has 3 words;

and the fourth line has 4 words.

The second and fourth lines should rhyme.

Choose some other words and write another form poem.

14 APPLY WITHIN

Name ....

Write an application to join the circus. What job would you apply for? List the skills that make you a suitable applicant.

Position applied for ....

Name ....

Date of Birth ....

Address ....

....

.... Postcode ....

School achievements ....

....

....

....

....

Work experience ....

....

....

....

....

....

Special skills ....

....

....

....

....

....

....

....

....

15 BUSINESS LETTER

Name....................

Use this format to write a business letter. You may wish to design your own letterhead for your company. If you are adding a letterhead you don't need to write out your company's address at the top of the letter.

....
....
....
....

....
....
....
....

....

....
....
....
....
....
....
....
....
....
....
....
....

....
....

16 FRED FLEETFOOT

Name . . . .

Design a comic strip using Fred Fleetfoot as the main character.

Where would Fred like to go?

What would a foot like Fred like to do?

The Adventures of Fred Fleetfoot

by . . . .

17 WORST DAY

Name . . . .

Finish this story.

I remember the worst day of my life well. It was a day that I hope never happens again. It all started when I . . . .

18 DELUXE HAMBURGER

Name.....................

Design your own ultimate hamburger.
Name it and list all the ingredients
that you would use.

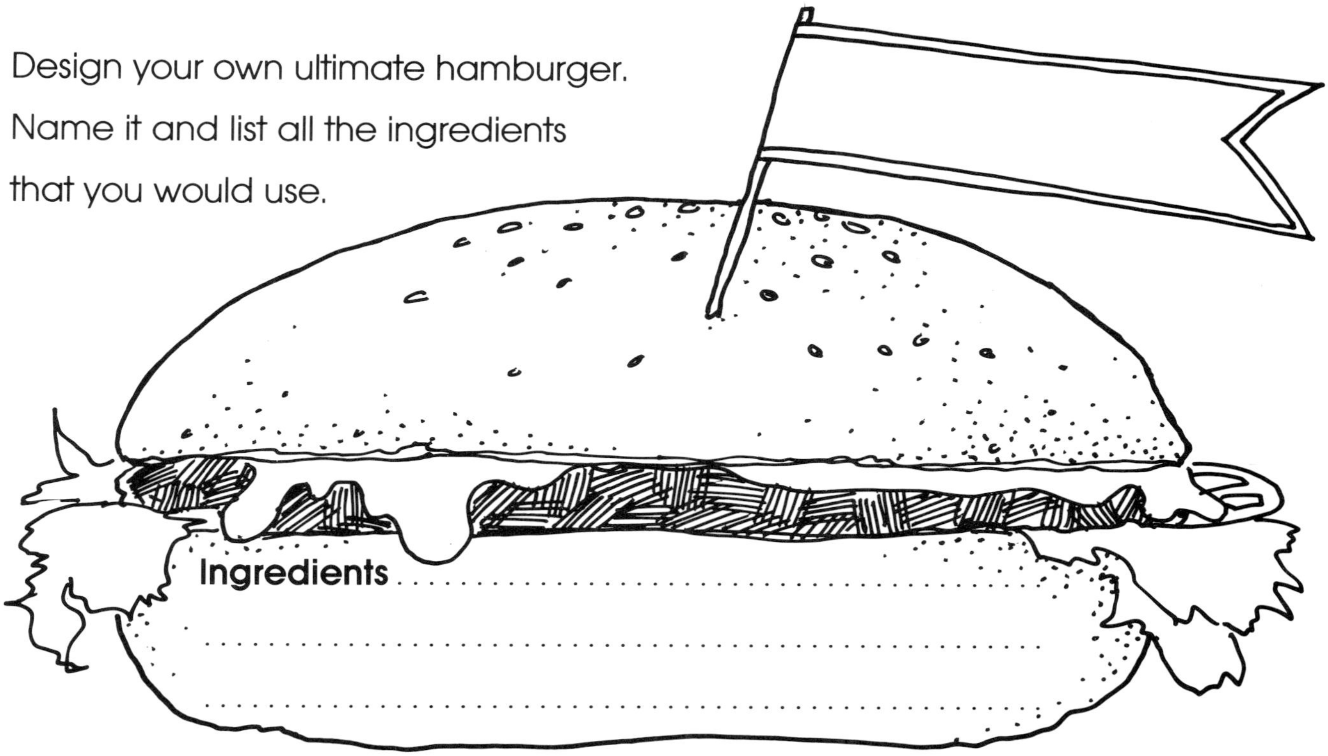

Write an eye-catching ad to put in the paper to introduce your wonderful new creation which will be available at an extra special introductory price this week.

19 MY COUNTRY

Name....................

When people think of Australia, different words and images appear.

What do you think of?

Use the letters of the word Australia to write a poem about your thoughts and feelings.

Each line must start with a word which begins with the letter shown.

MY COUNTRY

A ....

U ....

S ....

T ....

R ....

A ....

L ....

I ....

A ....

by ....

20 GUEST SPEAKER

Name....................

Your favourite sports star has been invited to speak to your class.

Write down three questions that you would like to ask.

1 ....

....

....

....

2 ....

....

....

....

3 ....

....

....

....

21 THIS WAY PLEASE

Name ....

Have you ever noticed how difficult it is to follow someone else's directions?

Write directions explaining how to get

To ....

From ....

Ask a friend to read your directions. How clear were they? ....

22 WINTER

Name. . . . .

Write two short paragraphs about Winter.

In Winter Wonders write about the things that you like in Winter.

In Winter Woes write about the things that you dislike in Winter.

. . . .

. . . .

. . . .

. . . .

. . . .

. . . .

. . . .

. . . .

. . . .

. . . .

. . . .

. . . .

. . . .

. . . .

. . . .

. . . .

23 OWNERS MANUAL

Name . . . .

My Pet

How to care for a . . . .

Things that you will need . . . .

Feeding . . . .

Cleaning . . . .

Grooming . . . .

Training . . . .

Sleeping . . . .

Health . . . .

24 WHAT NEXT?

Name. . . . .

A company that manufactures glass has announced a competition to find out the best use for an empty glass jar which is 20 cm high and has an 18 cm circumference.

Describe your idea and its applications to everyday life in no less than fifty words.

Run a class competition. Who can come up with the most uses? the funniest uses?

25 SPACE REPORT

Name. . . . .

You have been selected to travel to Mars. Publish a brief summary of the report that you wrote while you were on your journey.

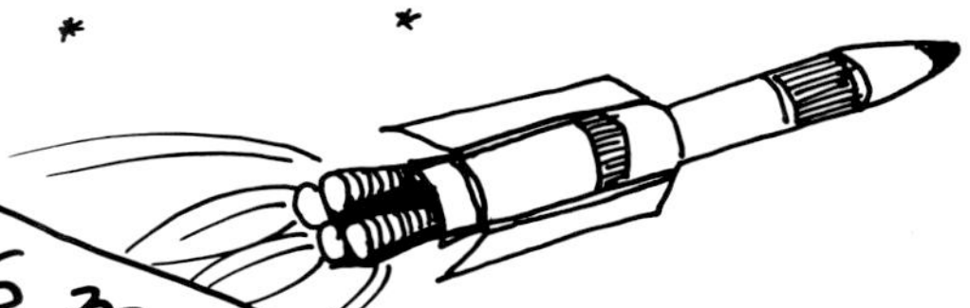

Early days

. . . .

. . . .

. . . .

. . . .

6 Months on

. . . .

. . . .

. . . .

. . . .

12 Months away

. . . .

. . . .

. . . .

. . . .

Mars!

. . . .

. . . .

. . . .

. . . .

Heading home

. . . .

. . . .

. . . .

. . . .

Earth at last

. . . .

. . . .

. . . .

. . . .

Use this as the basis for a longer story.

26 DEBATE THE ISSUE

Name....................

Should teachers have to wear school uniforms?

Write down all the reasons you can think of for and against this question.

Then design a uniform for your teacher.

For

....
....
....
....
....
....
....
....
....

Against

....
....
....
....
....
....
....
....
....

Teachers uniform

27 TRY EXERCISE

Name. . . . .

Write a 30 day exercise program to develop your muscles.

. . . .

28 BAD NEWS!

Name ....

Not all toys are safe. Which toy do you think should not be sold?

....

Why? ....

....

....

....

....

....

....

Write a letter to the paper to warn people about the dangers of the toy.

Dear Editor,

29 AN INVITATION

Name......................

Complete the details on the invitation below.

Remember to include the venue the date and the event.

30 A GREAT GAME

Name . . . .

Invent a game for 4-6 people to play.

It can be an indoor game or an outdoor game.

Equipment needed

. . . .

. . . .

. . . .

. . . .

. . . .

Rules

. . . .

. . . .

. . . .

. . . .

. . . .

. . . .

. . . .

Description of game

. . . .

. . . .

. . . .

. . . .

. . . .

. . . .

. . . .

31 A PASSING GRADE

Name . . . .

Write your own report. It can be fact or fiction. Fill in the report card below from your own point of view.

School . . . . Name . . . .

Reading	Completion of Assignments
Mathematics	
Spelling	Participation in Class
Written Expression	
Oral English	Consideration of Others
Handwriting	
Social Studies	
Science	Behaviour
Health and Physical Education	
Music	
Art and Craft	
Attendance	Punctuality

General Comments